To: _____

From: _____

Thanks be to God for his indescribable gift!

2 Corinthians 9:15 NIV

A garden is a friend you can visit anytime.

Every Gardener's
Journal

by Kimberly Montgomery

Published by J. Countryman,
a division of Thomas Nelson, Inc.,
Nashville, Tennessee 37214.

Project editor—Terri Gibbs

Designed by Left Coast Design Inc., Portland, Oregon.

ISBN: 08499-9513-2

Printed and bound in China

Every good and perfect gift is from above, and comes down from the Father of lights.

James 1:17

With all my love to Heather and Grace, the two most beautiful flowers in my garden.

One who plants a garden plants happiness. ♡

Gardening is a wonderful way to spend a life! Fragrant flowers in spring, fresh vegetables in summer, colorful leaves in fall, and the gentle blooms of bulbs in winter are just a few great reasons to spend time playing in the dirt. A popular hobby for generations, the sense of peace and serenity that comes from gardening is now more valuable then ever. As our lives become fuller and faster, it's wonderful to take time out and spend it among the flowers. I know that for me, even ten minutes of watering in the evening can improve my attitude. I'm always telling my husband (a non-gardener), "I don't _have_ to water, I get to water!"

There are many other rewards that come from gardening. Homegrown flowers to give to a friend or to decorate a holiday table. Fresh-off-the-vine ingredients for dinner. All the makings for potpourri drying in the cellar. I'm sure you have many more reasons why gardening is such a delight for you.

This journal was created to celebrate all the joys of gardening. Whether you have a few containers on a patio or several acres complete with an orchard, this book will help you along your way. There's space for plans and new ideas, a section for your very own to-do list, a place to make note of favorite plants and products, even a few pages for important resources and phone numbers. I hope you will use this as your gardening notebook—a place to be used and referred to often. Happy gardening!

My Garden Design

I find it helpful to have a rough sketch of the different areas of my garden. That way, if I want to make changes I can more easily see how the new designs will fit in with the existing plants. Use this space to plot out your own garden.

Gardening is a way of showing you believe in tomorrow.

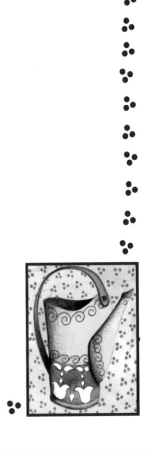

Garden Sketches

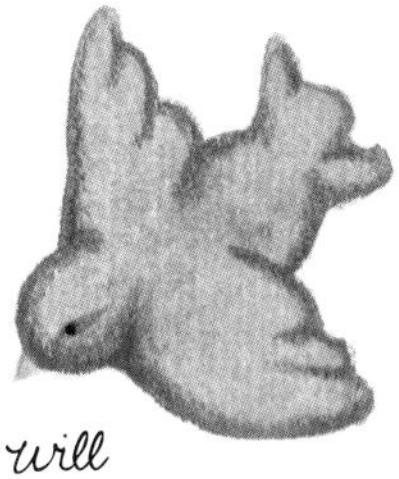

The Lord will
guide you continually,
and satisfy your soul
in drought...You shall
be like a watered garden.
Isaiah 58:11

Plants that are Growing in My Garden...

Trees

Shrubs

Herbs

- Herbs offer the greatest flavor and fragrance just as the first flower buds appear.
- As with most crops, it's best to harvest herbs early in the morning.
- To keep your herbs free of dust and bugs when drying, place a paper bag over each bundle. Make sure the herbs don't touch the sides of the bag, then tie with string.
- Herbs are dried and ready to be placed in jars when they crumble easily.
- Dill flowers make a beautiful garnish on a dinner plate.
- Always keep an Aloe Vera plant growing near the kitchen for use on burns.

V·E·G·E·T·A·B·L·E·S

-

Beets

-

Potatoes

-

Onions

-

Tomatoes

-

Zucchinni

- Cauliflower • Kale • Snap Peas • Radishes • Lettuce

Sal Lee's Saute

This delicious dish uses summer vegetables fresh from your garden. Serve it with roasted chicken and an herb bread for a great meal.

4 bacon strips
1 clove garlic, minced
1 onion, coarsely chopped
3 zucchini, sliced

3 crookneck squash, sliced
2 large tomatoes, chopped
1 C. shredded sharp cheddar cheese
salt and pepper to taste

Cook bacon in large non-stick frying pan until crisp. Remove from pan and drain. After bacon h as cooled, crumble into small pieces and set aside. In remaining bacon drippings saute garlic and onion over medium heat for 2 minutes. Add the squash and continue cooking until slightly tender. Reduce heat, add tomatoes and bacon, and gently stir to mix. Sprinkle with cheese, remove from heat and cover until cheese has melted. Serve immediately.

Serves 6

F·L·O·W·E·R·S

- Geranium
- Dianthus
- Poppy
- Morning Glory

Carnations • Sunflowers • Aster • Violets • Daylily

Pansies • Daliahs • Begonias • Roses • Snapdragon •

Alyssum • Zinnias • Petunias • Salvia • Marigolds • Daisy •

Lavender • Bluebells • Tulips • Daffodils • Crocus • Iris •

Roses

The world is a rose, smell it and pass it to your friends.
—Persian Proverb

Other Plants

·   ·

·   ·

·   ·

·   ·

·   ·

·   ·

·   ·

·   ·

·   ·

·   ·

·   ·

·   ·

·   ·

Big Plans

A new flowerbed or raised vegetable garden, a rose trellis on the front walk, an Old English style herb garden—what new plans are you thinking of? Here's the perfect place to keep track of all the ideas you pick up throughout the year. Make note of everything. You never know what may spark a great design in the future.

more Big Plans

_____

_____

_____

_____

_____

_____

_____

_____

_____

_____

_____

_____

There are no gardening mistakes, only experiments.

Janet Kilburn Phillips

Wish List

_____

_____

_____

_____

_____

_____

_____

_____

_____

_____

_____

_____

_____

_____

As the garden grows, so does the gardener.

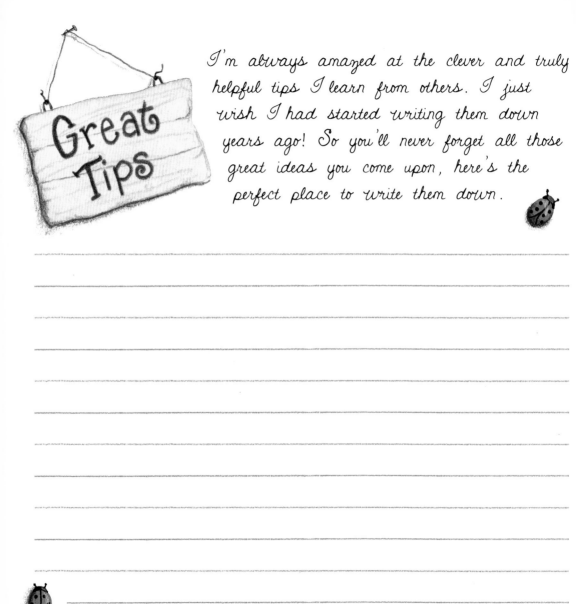

Great Tips

I'm always amazed at the clever and truly helpful tips I learn from others. I just wish I had started writing them down years ago! So you'll never forget all those great ideas you come upon, here's the perfect place to write them down.

Why didn't I think of that?

Planting

Feeding

A small garden will hold as much happiness as a big one. 🌼 Anonymous

Bug Control

Things ❀ To ❀ Do

Pruning, planting, seeding, watering, weeding—there's always plenty to do in the garden. However, with our lives so busy these days, it's easy to miss important dates in the garden. Make note here of all the tasks you want to accomplish throughout the seasons.

Winter

Spring

 Garden Angels gather here!

Zippidy DoDa

In spring, at the end of the day,
you should smell like dirt.

-Margaret Atwood

Summer

He who plants a seed in sod, believes in God.

Adam was a gardener, and God, who made him,
sees that half of all good gardening is done upon the knees.

-Rudyard Kipling

Fall

THIS YEAR

MY GARDEN

Use this space to record the happenings in your garden for the year. Note planting and flowering times, vegetable yields, bug problems and how you solved them, what worked and what didn't, and ideas you'd like to try next year.

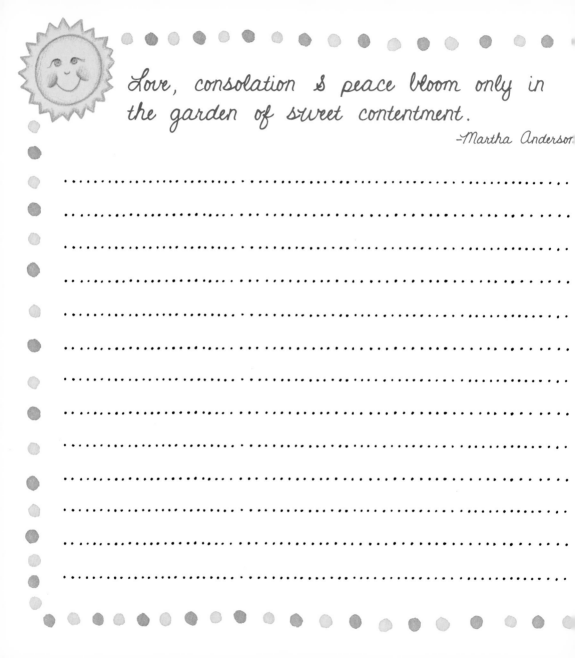

Love, consolation & peace bloom only in the garden of sweet contentment.

—Martha Anderson

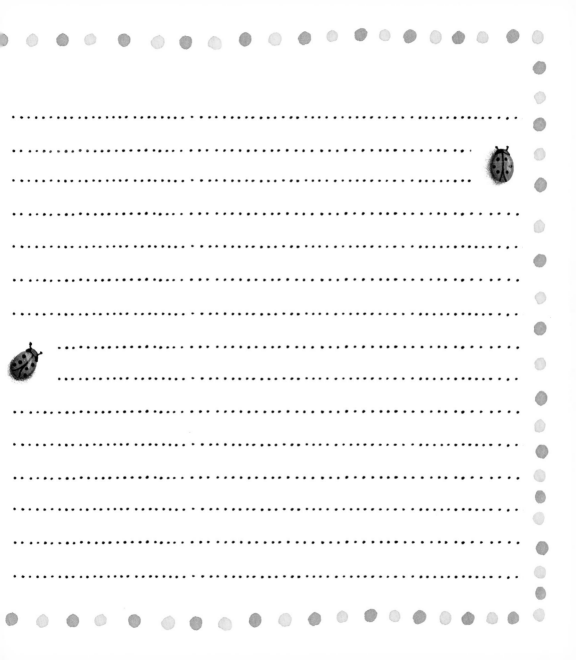

THYME BEGAN IN A GARDEN

If you would have a lovely garden, you should have a lovely life.

THE GARDENER'S MANUAL ~ 1843

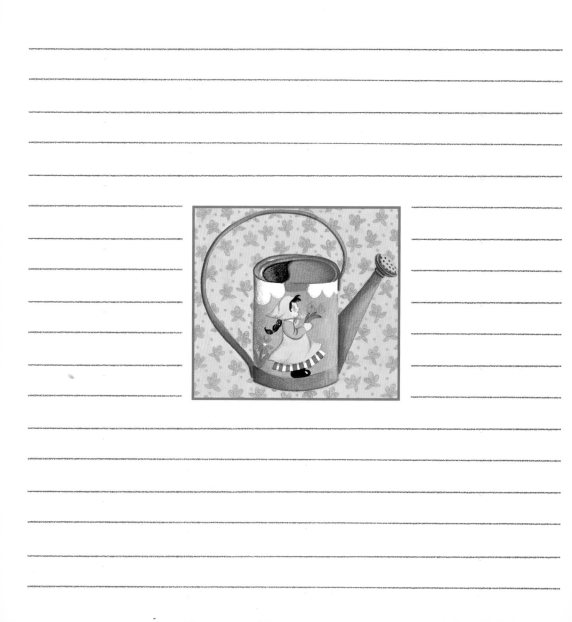

I planted the seed, God made it grow.

Garden Gift Ideas

....

....

....

....

....

....

....

....

....

....

....

....

....

....

....

Use this area to sketch your gift ideas.

· ·

· ·

· ·

· ·

· ·

· ·

· ·

· ·

· ·

· ·

· ·

· ·

*Little acts of
kindness are like flowers
along life's way.*
—Anonymous

· ·

· ·

· ·

· ·

· ·

more sketches

· ·
· ·
· ·
· ·
· ·
· ·
· ·
· ·
· ·
· ·
· ·
· ·
· ·
· ·
· ·
· ·
· ·

· ·

· ·

· ·

· ·

· ·

· ·

· ·

· ·

· ·

· ·

· ·

· ·

· ·

· ·

Our happiness is greatest when we ♥ contribute most to the happiness of others.

—Harriett Shipard

Gifts From My Garden

To: **What:** **When:**

_____ _____ _____

_____ _____ _____

_____ _____ _____

_____ _____ _____

_____ _____ _____

_____ _____ _____

_____ _____ _____

_____ _____ _____

_____ _____ _____

_____ _____ _____

To: What: When:

_____   _____   _____

_____   _____   _____

_____   _____   _____

_____   _____   _____

_____   _____   _____

_____   _____   _____

_____   _____   _____

_____   _____   _____

_____   _____   _____

_____   _____   _____

_____   _____   _____

_____   _____   _____

How Sweet!

To: What: When:

To: ....

What: ....

When: ....

Sow seeds of love and gather blessings of the Spirit.

Favorite Container Combinations

List combinations that have worked well and ones you'd like to try:

Favorite Cut-Flower *Combinations*

List cut-flower combinations that have worked well
and ones you'd like to try:

Record inspirational thoughts about your garden:

Reflections on my Garden

You can bury a lot of troubles by digging in the dirt.

You never know when someone
might catch a dream from you.

Gardens to Visit

Record gardens you'd like to visit—
locally or any place in the world!

_____

_____

_____

_____

_____

_____

_____

_____

_____

_____

_____

_____

_____

_____

General Garden Notes

General Garden Notes

Notes

Fun Facts

Vegetables need 6-8 hours of sunlight a day.

Bare root grapevines are available at most nurseries in February.

Early Girl is the most popular early season tomato.

A grandiflora rose is a cross between a floribunda
and a hybrid tea.

A Ladybug will eat its' weight in aphids daily.

Spreading dog hair throughout your garden
increases nitrogen in the soil.

A house wren feeds 500 bugs and caterpillars
to her babies every day.

Helpful Hints

Plant Amaryllis in October for holiday blooms.

The metal end of a retired rake makes a fun cup holder.

Only grow what you love to eat.

When creating a bouquet, match the flower color to the vase.

To speed the growth of Sweet Peas, soak seeds in thick paper towels 3-4 days before planting.

Use mulch to warm the soil for heat-loving crops.

Planting marigolds in the vegetable garden will greatly reduce bugs.

When planting bulbs, mark your trowel with finger nail polish at the depth you want to dig.

Notes

Arranging a bowl of flowers in the morning
can give a sense of quiet in a crowded day—
like writing a poem or saying a prayer.
—Ann Morrow Lindbergh

Notes

Play in the Dirt

B·E·S·T ❀ G·A·R·D·E·N ❀ P·R·O·D·U·C·T·S

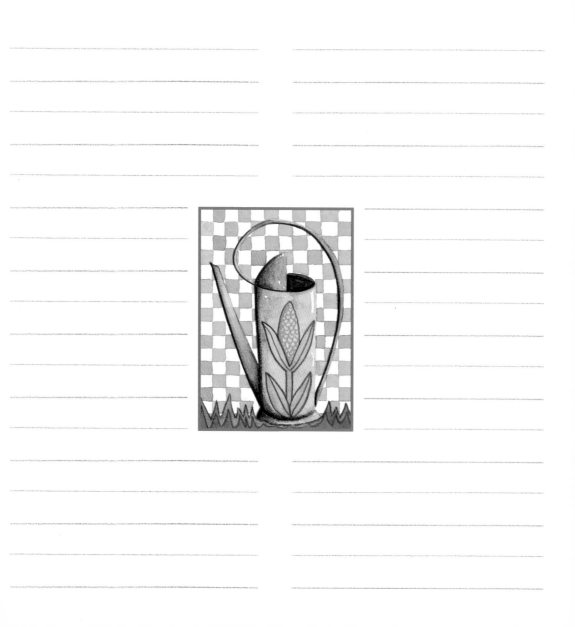

Garden Clubs

No woman should plant more garden than her husband can hoe.

Gardening Friends

Name: **Phone:**   **Address:**

· · · · · · · · · · · · · · ·   · · · · · · · · · · · · · · ·   · · · · · · · · · · · · · · ·

· · · · · · · · · · · · · · ·   · · · · · · · · · · · · · · ·   · · · · · · · · · · · · · · ·

· · · · · · · · · · · · · · ·   · · · · · · · · · · · · · · ·   · · · · · · · · · · · · · · ·

· · · · · · · · · · · · · · ·   · · · · · · · · · · · · · · ·   · · · · · · · · · · · · · · ·

· · · · · · · · · · · · · · ·   · · · · · · · · · · · · · · ·   · · · · · · · · · · · · · · ·

· · · · · · · · · · · · · · ·   · · · · · · · · · · · · · · ·   · · · · · · · · · · · · · · ·

· · · · · · · · · · · · · · ·   · · · · · · · · · · · · · · ·   · · · · · · · · · · · · · · ·

· · · · · · · · · · · · · · ·   · · · · · · · · · · · · · · ·   · · · · · · · · · · · · · · ·

· · · · · · · · · · · · · · ·   · · · · · · · · · · · · · · ·   · · · · · · · · · · · · · · ·

· · · · · · · · · · · · · · ·   · · · · · · · · · · · · · · ·   · · · · · · · · · · · · · · ·

· · · · · · · · · · · · · · ·   · · · · · · · · · · · · · · ·   · · · · · · · · · · · · · · ·

· · · · · · · · · · · · · · ·   · · · · · · · · · · · · · · ·   · · · · · · · · · · · · · · ·

· · · · · · · · · · · · · · ·   · · · · · · · · · · · · · · ·   · · · · · · · · · · · · · · ·

Name:

Phone:

Address:

Favorite ❀ Nurserys

Name: Phone: Specialty:

Name: **Phone:**   **Specialty:**

_____   _____   _____

_____   _____   _____

_____   _____   _____

_____   _____   _____

_____   _____   _____

_____   _____   _____

_____   _____   _____

_____   _____   _____

_____   _____   _____

_____   _____   _____

_____   _____   _____

Specialty Resources

Michael's Premier Roses
Owner: Michael Fischer
9759 Elder Creek Road
Sacramento, CA 95829
916-369-7673
www.michaelsrose.com

Michael grows over a thousand different roses and specializes in hard-to-find heirloom and miniature varieties. He's very helpful, knows all there is to know about roses, and ships year round.

Hortus Botanicus
Owner: Robert Goleman
20103 Hanson Road
Fort Bragg, CA 95437
707-964-4786
www.hortusb.com

This eclectic, collector's nursery is located down a country road in the Mendocino area of Northern California. Robert is warm and friendly and a storehouse of gardening information. He stocks a large collection of orchids, carnivorous plants, heirloom and Old English roses. (I bought some gorgeous tuberous begonias when I was there.)

Baylands Nursery
Owner: Day Boddorff
965 Weeks Street East
Palo Alto, CA 94303
650-323-1645
www.baylands.com

Day is a specialist in ornamental grasses and stocks over 50 kinds. He also carries a wide variety of day lilies and irises. He has a complete plant listing on this website and is currently working on a program for nationwide shipping.

Lee Valley Tools
Owner: Leonard Lee
12 East River Street
Ogdensburg, NY 13669
800-871-8158
www.leevalley.com

Lee designs and manufactures over 1000 high quality garden tools. His full color catalog carries a wide variety of useful and unique items for the gardener.

Helpful Websites

gardenweb.com

The premiere gardening website—featuring articles, products information, forums, calendar of events and more.

gardenguide.com

Tips, fun ideas, and special sections for vegetables, flowers and hers are just a few highlights of this site.

gardennet.com

This easy-to-use site is packed with specific information on every facet of gardening.

gardereview.com

This site was designed by gardeners for gardeners. A great place to research products and share information.

allaboutlawns.com

The name says it all—for the perfect lawn, check out this site first!

vg.com

The vg stands for Virtual Garden. This attractive site has good information and a lot of helpful links.

rose.org

This All American Rose Selection website contains just about everything you'll need to grow fabulous roses.

gardenersnet.com

Useful how-to-grow pages, fun ideas for the holidays, and a great kids section.

kimberlysgarden.com

Visit me on the web and leave me your favorite gardening tip or helpful hint!

I hope this journal has made your life in the garden more fun— and productive. It's been a joy writing, painting, and putting these pages together. Now it's time for me to get back out in the garden. I've got weeds to pull, roses to prune, tomatoes to pick, plants to feed, and I don't know how in the world that mint took over my basil pot.

Be well, be happy, and don't forget to water!

Happiness, like good soup, is always homemade.

Kimberly

DROP ME A NOTE WITH YOUR FAVORITE GARDENING IDEA ⁓ I'D LOVE TO HEAR FROM YOU!

KIMBERLY MONTGOMERY
4120 DOUGLAS BLVD. #306-170 · GRANITE BAY · CA 95746-5936